inspirational
journal

ReThink
YOUR
Life

wesleyan
publishing
house

Indianapolis, Indiana

Contents

Introduction

No one disputes the importance of eating the right way and getting plenty of exercise. The more healthy your lifestyle the better you will feel on a daily basis and the longer you will live. In other words, healthy eating leads to a higher quality of life. However, we know that if we choose to live a sedentary lifestyle and feed our body all kinds of junk, we will pay the price for that way of life. We know this to be true even if we fail to live out the truth in our own lives.

In comparison, few people today seem to understand the importance of having a healthy diet for your mind. Our minds are bombarded with all kinds of unhealthy messages and images on a daily basis. We must be proactive about avoiding destructive thoughts and feeding our minds a healthy diet of truth or we will pay the price of an unhealthy, unfit thought life. If we are to live and grow as Jesus' disciples, we must avoid the deception and lies of the Enemy and allow our minds and hearts to be shaped by the truth of the gospel.

The introduction to *ReThink Your Life: A Unique Diet to Renew Your Mind** makes the statement that, "The key to controlling your life is to control your mind," and that we need to care for our minds in order to lead "happy, healthy, productive lives."

The Bible certainly addresses the importance of right thinking as it relates to quality of life, and especially the quality of our spiritual life. In the days before the flood, God looked upon the despicable deeds human beings were committing, and he traced those deeds to their wicked thoughts. Genesis 6:5 says, "The LORD saw how great man's wickedness on the earth had become, and that every inclination of the thoughts of his heart was only evil all the time."

Many Bible teachers compare the immorality, irreverence, and injustices of modern times with pre-flood times. It is easy to understand their reasoning. Daily, the media reports a long list of crimes and scandals that reach all the way from our communities to our government. Several prominent religious leaders have fallen into scandalous sin. Clearly, believers must guard their minds against the harmful influences of a corrupt culture; fill their minds with godly thoughts; and put what they learn into wholesome, productive practices.

In his letter to the Philippians, Paul warned his readers about the ungodly lifestyle of enemies of the cross (Phil. 3:18–19). He also urged his readers to think about "whatever is true, whatever is noble, whatever is right, whatever is pure, whatever is lovely, whatever is admirable . . . excellent or praiseworthy" (4:8). Further, he told them to put into practice what he had taught them by precept and example (4:9). Right thinking and right living are inseparable companions.

But Paul wasn't the only apostle to stress the importance of the mind. After mentioning the benefits of the prophets' and apostles' words, the apostle Peter wrote, "Therefore, prepare your minds for action" (1 Pet. 1:13).

This journal will help you to rethink your way to a productive, joyful life. Along the way, you will encounter daily entries. Each entry is designed with a theme, a key Bible verse, an inspirational story, a few statements or questions to help you record your thoughts, a recommended action you can take, and a prayer to echo.

I hope you enjoy every step of the journey!

NOTE

*Stan Toler, *ReThink Your Life: A Unique Diet to Renew Your Mind* (Indianapolis, Ind.: Wesleyan Publishing House, 2008), 12. This inspirational journal is a companion book to *ReThink Your Life*.

Detoxification

The Origin of Wrong Thinking

ENGAGE

Wrong thinking predates human history. It began in the mind of Lucifer, a prominent light-bearing angel. He determined to topple God from his throne and take his place. He reasoned, "I will ascend to heaven; I will raise my throne above the stars of God; I will sit enthroned . . . I will make myself like the Most High" (Isa. 14:13–14). But the coup failed; God cast Lucifer down to the earth.

Where did wrong thinking begin?

TODAY'S VERSE

"For everyone who exalts himself will be humbled, and he who humbles himself will be exalted" (Luke 14:11).

EXAMINE

A preacher told his congregation about a little boy who announced to his father that he was nine feet tall.

The boy's father asked, "What makes you think you are nine feet tall, Jimmy?"

Little Jimmy removed a shoe and measured himself with it. "See, Daddy, I'm nine feet tall."

Then the father removed his size eleven shoe, handed it to Jimmy, and said, "Use this shoe to measure yourself."

Suddenly, little Jimmy had shrunk closer to his correct size.

Jesus desires and expects to be Lord of the way you think.

Humans often think they are bigger than they really are. A highly educated person may glory in his academic degrees. A successful businessman may take full credit for his accomplishments. An athlete may boast about his prowess on the court, track, course, ice, or gridiron. A rich person may gloat that he gained his wealth without anybody else's help. A musician may bask in self-glory as an audience exclaims, "Bravo!"

True greatness, however, is measured by our humility, and we are truly humble when we think of God's greatness and our need to depend on him.

EXPLORE

Sinful pride springs from wrong thinking. If we think we do not need God or we are capable of accomplishing our goals without God or we are worthy of worship, our thinking needs to undergo detoxification.

What thoughts about yourself do you need to correct with God's help?

> He that is humble ever shall have God to be his guide.
>
> —John Bunyan

EXERCISE

Write down one way you will serve someone humbly today. For example, you may wish to assist an elderly neighbor in some way or visit a nursing home resident or run an errand for a sick person.

PRAY

Father, may my thoughts of you be pleasing in your sight, and may I not think more highly of myself than I ought to think.

Satan's Sneaky Attack on the Mind

We can almost hear the serpent's hiss in each temptation.

ENGAGE

Having been evicted from his permanent residence in heaven, Lucifer, also known as the Dragon, the Devil, Satan, and that ancient serpent (Rev. 20:2), approached Eve in the garden of Eden. He wanted her and Adam to sin, and he employed a successful strategy; he attacked Eve's thinking. He caused her to doubt God's words. He wanted her to think God was unfair. He said God had lied about the consequence of disobeying him (see Gen. 3:1–4).

TODAY'S VERSE

"Put on the full armor of God so that you can take your stand against the devil's schemes" (Eph. 6:11).

EXAMINE

Contrary to popular cartoon depictions of the Devil, he doesn't have horns and a pointy tail. Nor does he carry a pitchfork. He is far too cunning to present himself as a sinister character. Often, he employs the services of men and women who appear wise, gentle, and trusting. The Devil's bait appears to be sweet, but his trap closes viciously. It is essential, therefore, to program our minds with Scripture so we will be able to discern right from wrong.

> Every temptation is an opportunity of our getting nearer to God.
> —John Quincy Adams

A seminary student considered a professor personable, kind, and wise until the professor smiled and said, "Jesus was not truly God. He was simply a model human being, and a perfect example of love." The student knew the Bible well enough to realize the professor's thinking was wrong, and he was shocked by the professor's words. Furthermore, the student remembered a hymn he had often sung at church. His mind replayed the words: "I will not trust the sweetest frame, but wholly lean on Jesus' name. On Christ, the Solid Rock I stand. All other ground is sinking sand."

Someone who seems so trustworthy may aid the Devil in his sneaky scheme to deceive us. Our best line of defense is to store Scripture in our minds and hearts.

EXPLORE

What have you heard recently that contradicts the teaching of God's Word?

Thought is not powerless: It creates an atmosphere that hinders or helps.

—author unknown

Why do you agree or disagree that the Devil uses sneaky means to accomplish his purposes?

What is your opinion of the advice, "If it feels good, it must be right"?

EXERCISE

Choose one of the following Scriptures to memorize today: Psalm 1:1–2; 119:11; Matthew 4:10. Share what you memorize with a friend or family member.

PRAY

Father, guided by your Word and empowered by your Spirit, may I resist temptation and walk in paths of righteousness.

Day 3

GIGO:
Garbage In, Garbage Out

Our lives are the products of our thinking.

ENGAGE

We live in an environmentally conscious age. Concern about toxins in our water supply, our food, and even the air is widespread. However, less concern seems to be focused on what we feed our minds. In computer language, GIGO means "Garbage In, Garbage Out." The term serves well as a reminder that the corrupt things we put into our thinking will manifest themselves in our conduct.

TODAY'S VERSE

"For out of the heart come evil thoughts, murder, adultery, sexual immorality, theft, false testimony, slander" (Matt. 15:19).

EXAMINE

A door-to-door salesman claimed to be conducting an environmental survey. "I know you are a busy person, but the survey will take only a few minutes," he explained when I answered the door.

I consented.

He asked, "How clean do you think our air is? Very clean, fairly clean, or not clean at all?"

Quickly, he moved to a similar question about our tap water. "Do you think it is pure, fairly pure, or not pure at all?"

> It is a big sin to give sanctuary to even a little sinful thought.
>
> —author unknown

Soon it became clearer than air that he was selling a water purification system.

Perhaps our water supply isn't 100 percent pure and drinking it may lead to health problems, but I wasn't concerned enough to buy the salesman's product. I think my city's water is just fine.

I do know, however, that mind pollution is a global reality. Watching immoral movies and TV shows, reading racy novels and magazines, listening to off-color jokes, and harboring illicit fantasies produce bad behavior, just as a bad tree produces bad fruit (Matt. 7:17–18).

How free of toxins is your mind?

EXPLORE

None of us would intentionally drink from a dirty glass or eat with a dirty knife and fork, so shouldn't we be just as cautious about what touches our minds? Why is it hard to keep the mind pure? How can you displace impure thoughts with pure thoughts?

What's worse than having a junky body? Having a junky mind.

EXERCISE

What TV shows or kinds of movies are injurious to a spiritual mindset? List them, and discard the list in a trash can as you decide to strike them from your life.

PRAY

Father, I want to rid my mind of what is impure and unholy. Help me to think on things that please and honor you.

Day 4

Universal Blackout

ENGAGE

You may have experienced a blackout, a power outage that left you and your neighbors in the dark for several hours or days. Blackouts are frustrating but not rare. They can occur anywhere and in any season. Floods, wind, a heavy snow, lightning, or an energy drain can cause a blackout. However, a blackout has never been worldwide— or has it?

Bats live in dark caves, but human beings were not created to live in the darkness. Nevertheless, the minds of millions of people are void of spiritual light.

TODAY'S VERSE

"The god of this age has blinded the minds of unbelievers, so that they cannot see the light of the gospel of the glory of Christ, who is the image of God" (2 Cor. 4:4).

EXAMINE

In his youth, John Newton (1725–1807) served on a slave ship that took him to Sierra Leone. He experienced abuse at the hands of a slave trader until a sea captain who had known his father rescued him. Eventually, John became captain of his own slave ship.

> Every soul not already won to Jesus is already lost.
>
> —James Gray

During a violent storm, John feared for his life as he tried to steer his ship to safety. When all seemed lost, he called upon the Lord for deliverance. Later in his cabin, he reflected on God's grace and described his conversion in his beloved hymn, "Amazing Grace." In that hymn, he testifies, "I once was lost, but now am found, was blind, but now I see." For the rest of his life, he identified May 10, 1748, as the day of his conversion.

John Newton left the slave trade and became a minister of the gospel. The Holy Spirit swept the darkness from his mind.

EXPLORE

What evidence of spiritual blindness do you see in the world today?

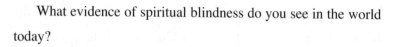

Is the unbelieving, Harvard lawyer as spiritually blind as the pagan, witch doctor? Why or why not?

How did Newton come to the light of salvation?

EXERCISE

Record the name of one unbelieving friend or coworker who needs Christ. Pray for that person today, and also share the enlightening gospel with him or her.

O Thou to Whose all searching sight
The darkness shineth as the light,
Search, prove my heart; it pants for Thee;
O burst these bonds, and set it free!

—John Wesley

PRAY

Father, I thank you for lifting the darkness from my mind. Empower me by your Spirit to share the light of the gospel with someone today.

Day 5

Lights On!

ENGAGE

My wife and I rode the rails from Chicago to Seattle in 1993. The scenery was delightful, and the engineer was kind enough to stop the train at Glacier National Park and allow the passengers to step out and breathe the park's pure air. But one section of the route was neither scenic nor invigorating. We passed through a tunnel in Montana that was 7.79 miles long—and densely dark. Everyone seemed elated when we emerged from the tunnel and entered the light of a glorious day. Leaving spiritual darkness behind and entering the light of salvation is an even better experience.

What a relief it is to see the lights go on after a blackout, but it is an occasion of great joy when light dispels darkness from the mind and heart.

TODAY'S VERSE

"I am the light of the world. Whoever follows me will never walk in darkness, but will have the light of life" (John 8:12).

EXAMINE

He despised Jesus, and he hated Christians. Steeped in religious legalism and ritualism, Saul of Tarsus was blind to his lost condition. He assumed his racial heritage, his devotion to the law of Moses, his identification as a strict Pharisee, and his religious zeal earned him God's favor. But he was so wrong and so blind to the truth.

> For you were once darkness, but now you are light in the Lord. Live as children of light.
>
> —Ephesians 5:8

One day he learned how wrong and blind he was. On that day, he met Jesus, the risen Lord and the light of the world.

Saul's heart was burning with the desire to arrest followers of Jesus in Damascus and haul them to Jerusalem for punishment. He did not know that on the way to Damascus, Jesus would find him, apprehend him, and change the course of his life.

As Saul approached Damascus, a light from heaven blinded him. He fell to the ground and heard Jesus call to him. Jesus identified himself and instructed Saul to enter Damascus, where he would receive further instructions. Saul obeyed. The Lord he had persecuted had suddenly become the Lord he would serve. Saul became the apostle Paul, who spread the light of the gospel throughout the Roman Empire.

EXPLORE

A mind blinded by Satan cannot perceive spiritual truth (1 Cor. 2:14). How did your perception of spiritual truth change when you became a believer? How does the Holy Spirit help you share the good news?

> The commands of the LORD are radiant, giving light to the eyes.
> —Psalm 19:8

EXERCISE

After believing in Jesus, Saul (Paul) obeyed the Lord's instructions. Read Ephesians 4:1–3 and 17–30, and list commands you find there. Place a checkmark beside each one as you obey it.

PRAY

Thank you, Father, for delivering me from spiritual darkness. Strengthen me by your Spirit to walk daily in the light and to guide others to the light of the world.

Day 6

What's on Your Mind?

ENGAGE

Ranchers build fences to keep their cattle and horses from straying, and they inspect those fences regularly to mend any section that has fallen down. Christians ought to secure their minds to retain appropriate thoughts and to fence out destructive thoughts.

TODAY'S VERSE

"You will keep in perfect peace him whose mind is steadfast, because he trusts in you" (Isa. 26:3).

EXAMINE

A casual observer of Charles lying in a hospital bed might have wondered why he was there. He looked fine, and a big smile lit up his face. A closer glance, though, would detect a tube extending from a machine to Charles's side. He had lung cancer. The machine was pumping air into his lungs, and as soon as the tube was removed, Charles would die.

Was Charles worried? Not in the least. He would tell you he was "fine, praise the Lord." If you asked how his day was going, he would say, "I'm having a good day. Every day with the Lord is a good day, but some are better than others."

He kept a supply of gospel tracts beside his bed, handed them to doctors, nurses, staff members, and visitors. He wanted them to enjoy the same peace of mind he possessed as a believer whose mind was steadfastly focused on the Lord.

> If you want to be miserable, worry. If you want to be happy, trust.
> —author unknown

After the attending doctor removed the air hose from Charles' side, Charles told his wife he loved her. He kissed her one last time, said goodbye, and slipped into the presence of Christ.

EXPLORE

Circle the word that best describes your current peace of mind:

nonexistent   shaky   fairly strong   perfect

What anxieties, if any, seem to trouble you repeatedly?

What Bible promises have helped you to rid your mind of worry?

EXERCISE

Discuss the issue of worry with a Christian friend and pray together, casting your cares on Jesus.

PRAY

Father, I commit my anxieties to you. I know that no problem is too big for you to handle. Fill my mind with your peace today, and increase my faith.

Day 7

A Diet for the Mind

ENGAGE

"For most people . . . as much as you like your media intake, you don't necessarily need most of what you imbibe . . . just like you don't need dessert with every meal, chances are you can get by with consuming far less media than you currently do" (*ReThink Your Life*, 53).

Flooding the mind with media images and messages is a sure way to become spiritually flabby. Is it time to put the mind on a diet?

TODAY'S VERSE

"Love the Lord your God with all your heart and with all your soul and with all your mind" (Matt. 22:37).

> Greatly reduce the amount of data you consume, and with the time you save, renew your focus on the Creator of your mind.

EXAMINE

Have you noticed that TV weight-loss commercials gang up on viewers at the beginning of a new year? The reason is obvious: from Thanksgiving through Christmas, people pile on the pounds by eating far too much. When they sneak a glance at the scales on New Year's Day, they think, "My first resolution of the year is to lose weight." Weight-loss programs and gyms tap into this aspiration by launching commercials that promise fun, easy ways to slim down, but the good intentions and the commercials fade out after a few weeks.

Let's face it—it's hard to lose weight. Unless a person makes up his or her mind to do so and maintains an unyielding mental discipline, the pounds will creep back. But ongoing mental discipline pays off in terms of better health and personal appearance.

Maintaining a sensible diet of the mind pays off too. If we overload our minds on messages from such media as TV, movies, Facebook, Twitter, Blackberries, iPhones, iPods, iPads, and other devices, we can become media junkies. Taking time to feed our minds with God's Word is the way to grow spiritually healthy, strong, and vibrant.

EXPLORE

How much time do you spend each day . . .

- watching TV or movies?

- surfing the Internet?

- reading the newspaper?

- playing video games?

- receiving text messages, e-mails, Tweets (Twitter), and Facebook messages?

- reading the Bible?

Are you willing to go on a media fast? Why or why not?

EXERCISE

Put your mind on a diet today by not turning on the TV or reading a newspaper. Instead, read an entire book of the Bible.

PRAY

Father, I don't want to overindulge on media messages; I want to feed on your word. As I read your Word today, enlighten my mind so that I will be spiritually fit for your service.

Realignment

Personal Pity Party

ENGAGE

In some parts of the world, people try to atone for their sins by thrashing their backs until they bleed. Others lie on beds of nails or crawl on their knees up a steep incline of many concrete steps. Unfortunately, some Christians beat themselves up—they don't thrash themselves; they trash themselves verbally. They don't crawl on their knees up concrete steps; they make their skin crawl by ingesting nasty self-accusations.

If we focused on God's grand purpose for us, we would celebrate rather than commiserate.

TODAY'S VERSE

"For it is God who works in you to will and to act according to his good purpose" (Phil. 2:13).

EXAMINE

Do you ever host a pity party for yourself? "Been there, done that," you say. Who hasn't? At one time or another, each of us gets down on ourselves. We think we are useless, ugly, stupid, a loser, or some other highly uncomplimentary kind of poor soul. But guess what? God doesn't see us like that, and fortunately, he doesn't give up on us and toss us onto the nearest scrap pile.

How precious to me are your thoughts, O God! How vast is the sum of them!

—Psalm 139:17

The prophet Elijah held a pity party for himself in the middle of a desolate wilderness. First Kings 19:4 reports that he even prayed that the Lord would take his life. He felt like a colossal failure. "I am no better than my ancestors," he lamented.

But God didn't end Elijah's life. Instead, he gave him a new lease on life, a new vision of himself, and new assignments. God was still at work in Elijah's life, and God is at work in yours too.

EXPLORE

Have you noticed a variety in God's people? Some are good-looking; others are not. Some are talented; others are not. Some are good speakers; others are not. But every believer is precious to God, and he is working in every believer's life to accomplish his purpose. How does knowing these facts encourage you?

EXERCISE

Look in the mirror today, and say, "God loves me, and I can serve him today."

List a few positive differences God has brought into your life since you became a believer.

> Closer is He than breathing, and nearer than hands and feet.
>
> —Alfred Tennyson

PRAY

Father, I praise you for your great love. Help me to see myself as you see me. May the Holy Spirit empower me to be all that you want me to be today.

A Good Attitude

If we are tempted to feel defeated, it is time for a new attitude.

ENGAGE

Often the difference between gloom and optimism depends on one's attitude. One patient with a terminal illness may believe she is doomed to a brief time of misery followed by death. Another woman with a similar illness resolves to triumph over it. She greets each day with optimism, endures pain, looks on the sunny side of life, and seizes every opportunity to be cheerful and useful.

TODAY'S VERSE

"Rejoice in the Lord always. I will say it again: Rejoice!" (Phil. 4:4).

EXAMINE

Two cancer patients were in the same hospital. They were only three rooms apart, but their attitudes were poles apart. Although both were believers, they responded differently to the news that cancer had invaded their bodies. Fred, who had been diagnosed with stomach cancer, blamed his affliction on the Lord. Meg, who had been diagnosed with leukemia of the bones, committed her affliction to the Lord.

> Sometimes we succumb to feelings of abandonment; we feel isolated, as though we're the only ones who have ever gone through what we're facing and God doesn't hear us.

Fred grumbled and complained. Meg praised the Lord.

Fred seemed reluctant to pray or even have others pray for him. Meg welcomed prayer. With a big smile, she said that she had heard from Christians as far away as South America who said they were praying for her. "I am so blessed," she said.

EXPLORE

Romans 8:28 promises that "in all things God works for the good of those who love him." How do you reconcile the teaching of this verse with the so-called "bad things" that have happened to you?

How have you seen the benefits of a good attitude in your life or someone else's life?

Often the difference between defeat and victory depends on one's attitude.

—author unknown

EXERCISE

If you need an attitude adjustment, have a talk with Jesus today. If a friend, coworker, or neighbor's attitude needs a lift, encourage him or her today with a cheerful phone call, card, or visit.

PRAY

Father, I confess I have felt gloomy lately. Please forgive me, and help me joyfully accept whatever you bring into my life. Help me spread your joy to others.

Day 3

Snatching Victory from the Jaws of Defeat

ENGAGE

Who hasn't seen a football team play poorly in the first half and trail by at least twenty points? The losing team shuffles off to the locker room with their heads hanging down. But the second half is entirely different. The same players score more than three touchdowns and keep the opponents from scoring—and they win the game. They have snatched victory from the jaws of defeat. But how? The answer is they heeded their coach's halftime instructions.

We may feel defeated and ready to give up, but if we turn matters over to the Lord, defeat will turn to victory.

TODAY'S VERSE

"I can do everything through him who gives me strength" (Phil. 4:13).

EXAMINE

Simon, Andrew, James, and John must have felt defeated. They had fished all night but hadn't caught any fish. That was a disastrous situation. After all, for those four men, fishing wasn't a sport; it was their livelihood. "Will Fish for Food" wasn't a sign they held at a busy intersection; it was their way of life. We can understand, then, that they were ready to hang it up and go home empty-handed when Jesus approached.

More than conquerors
through Him who loved us,
Read the promise o'er and o'er;
Not almost or very nearly,
But conquerors and more.

—Lillian M. Weeks

While the four fishermen were washing their nets, Jesus entered Simon's boat, asked him to push out a little, and then sat down and taught the people gathered on the shore. Afterward, he instructed Simon to navigate into deep water and drop his nets for a catch of fish.

At first, Simon objected because he and his partners had worked hard all night without catching anything. But he obeyed Jesus, and, suddenly, so many fish swam into the nets that they began to break. A night of defeat had turned to victory because the fishermen did what Jesus commanded.

Instead of feeling defeated by difficult circumstances, we can be more than conquerors through Jesus.

EXPLORE

What circumstances seem to be crushing your spirit today?

Will you surrender those circumstances to Jesus?

Why do you agree or disagree that defeatism is a product of self-reliance instead of reliance on the Lord?

EXERCISE

Today, identify two negative thoughts you will dispel, and replace with reliance on the Lord.

What ministry have you recently abandoned that you will resume with reliance on the Lord?

If there be no enemy, no fight; if no fight, no victory; if no victory, no crown.

—Savonarola

PRAY

Father, without Jesus, I can do nothing. But I can do everything through him. Help me claim victory in Jesus.

Day 4

Bask in God's Love

ENGAGE

Many people have a hard time accepting God's love; they think they must earn it or buy it. So they slavishly perform religious deeds and place a generous check in Sunday's offering plate. But neither a lifetime of religious works nor all the gold in Fort Knox can gain God's love. Like the air we breathe, God's love surrounds us, and it is free.

The fact that God loves you and me is astounding, amazing, and true.

TODAY'S VERSE

"How great is the love the Father has lavished on us, that we should be called children of God!" (1 John 3:1).

EXAMINE

"I don't believe God can love me." A homeless person had entered a Chicago rescue mission and heard me tell the audience that God loved everyone. He met me after the service to tell me God could not possibly love him. "I have done some terrible things in my life," he explained, "and I've been in and out of jail so many times I've lost count."

"You may not love yourself," I responded, "but I know God loves you."

"What makes you so sure?" he asked.

I replied, "He sent his Son to die for your sins and mine and for the sins of the whole world. When he lived on earth, he accepted and forgave all kinds of people—even people that others rejected: thieves, prostitutes, lepers, and demon-possessed people. He turned no one away. Even a man who was hateful, violent, and an accomplice to murder became a brand-new person when he accepted God's love. His name was Saul of Tarsus. Here's something he wrote after he became a believer in Jesus."

> He loves you, not because of anything you do; he loves you simply because you are his child.

I opened my Bible to Romans 5:8 and read, "God demonstrates his own love for us in this: While we were still sinners, Christ died for us."

The man got it. He opened his heart to God's love, and believed in Jesus.

EXPLORE

What words would you use to describe God's love?

How has God's love made your life meaningful?

Do you believe God loves some people more than others? Why or why not?

EXERCISE

Read 1 Corinthians 13 today, and substitute the word *God* for each mention of *love*.

Tell at least one person today that God loves him or her.

> To write the love of God above
> Would drain the ocean dry;
> Nor could the scroll contain the whole,
> Though stretched from sky to sky.
>
> —Frederick M. Lehman

PRAY

I love you, Lord, because you first loved me. Let me bask in your love and be a channel of it.

Day 5

Confession:
Instant Weight Loss

Confession is a glorious thing. Why? Because God already knows what you've done! He can hardly wait for you to tell him about it and ask for forgiveness.

ENGAGE

Obesity is a significant national problem that affects not only adults but children too. Obesity is a potential killer. It puts the heart and kidneys at risk, and it increases the risk of diabetes. Unfortunately, there is no quick way to drop excess weight. But quickly losing a weight of guilt is an entirely different matter.

TODAY'S VERSE

"If we confess our sins, he is faithful and just and will forgive us our sins and purify us from all unrighteousness" (1 John 1:9).

EXAMINE

According to the *Guinness World Records*, an American woman, Rosalie Bradford, lost 907 pounds, and a British man, Jon Brower Minnoch, lost 924 pounds. After losing so much weight, they must have felt not only elated but also infused with boundless energy. Reaching one's weight-loss goal is a reason to celebrate, as anyone knows who has watched *The Biggest Loser* TV show.

Wouldn't it be nice if a pharmaceutical company developed a harmless, inexpensive pill that would get rid of excess weight with just one swallow? I suppose we can dream on.

There is tremendously good news for those who need to get rid of a load of guilt immediately and once for all. God has prescribed confession—not a simple, meaningless "I'm sorry" mantra, but a sincere, repentant, heartfelt, urgent admission of guilt and request for God's forgiveness.

King David was a deeply troubled man after committing adultery and arranging for his mistress's husband-soldier to be killed in action. Even his bones seemed to break under a crushing load of sin and guilt. But he confessed his sin, and God forgave him (read Pss. 51 and 32).

> The world has lost the power to blush over its vice; the Church has lost her power to weep over it.
>
> —Leonard Ravenhill

No sin is too big for God to lift and cast into the sea of his forgetfulness!

EXPLORE

How can God forgive sin?

Are you guilty of covering a sin?

If so, how is that cover-up affecting your relationship with God and others?

I couldn't live in peace if I put the shadow of a willful sin between myself and God.

—George Eliot

How do you feel when you confess a sin and God forgives you?

EXERCISE

On a sheet of paper, write a sin that you need to confess. Now, confess that sin, thank God for forgiving the sin and lifting your guilt. Crumple the sheet of paper, and toss "the sin" into a trash can.

PRAY

"I said, 'I will confess my transgressions to the LORD'—and you forgave the guilt of my sin" (Ps. 32:5).

Day 6

You Are Royalty

A Christian is a member of God's royal family.

ENGAGE

A popular TV show in the 1950s, *Queen for a Day*, featured four women with sob stories who were interviewed by Jack Bailey. The audience chose by loudest applause the woman who would be crowned queen for a day and have her wish fulfilled. For one day, she moved out of difficult circumstances and enjoyed royal treatment. Believers have moved from the poverty and domination of sin into God's royal family. They enjoy his unrivaled love and kindness forever.

TODAY'S VERSE

"He has taken me to the banquet hall, and his banner over me is love" (Song 2:4).

EXAMINE

How would you feel living in isolation, fear, and dependence on others? Mephibosheth lived in a desert. He had been lame for almost his entire life, and he assumed his life was in jeopardy. Would King David kill him because he was a grandson of Saul, who had tried many times to kill David?

What must have gone through Mephibosheth's mind when David's men found him and brought him to David? Total apprehension! But David quickly alleviated Mephibosheth's fear. He showed him kindness by awarding him property, servants, and the privilege of dining daily with King David. Best of all, he conferred honorary royal sonship on him, "Mephibosheth ate at David's table like one of the king's sons" (2 Sam. 9:11).

In the first three chapters of Ephesians, you'll find a list of the blessings God gives his children. Not because we're good— just because we're his.

There is no reason to disparage yourself. You can dismiss any feeling of worthlessness or insignificance. God has adopted you into his royal family, and he has set a table for you in his banquet hall. Thank him for such kindness, and fellowship with him daily.

EXPLORE

If you were to compose a certificate verifying your spiritual birth, what would you write?

Why does membership in God's royal family give you a positive self-image and a positive outlook on life?

Do not be afraid, little flock, for your Father has been pleased to give you the kingdom.

—Luke 12:32

EXERCISE

Write a letter or send an e-mail to a non-Christian friend in which you cite the benefits of belonging to God's family.

PRAY

Father, thank you for including me in your royal family. Help me appreciate the worth you have attached to me by calling me your child.

That's What Friends Are For

ENGAGE

Good parents want their children to surround themselves with good friends. They know bad friends can exert heavy peer pressure to do bad things. However, adult peer pressure is real too. If an adult builds a circle of close friends whose habits are bad, he or she may become like them. A wise Christian will cultivate godly friendships.

Good Christian friends are God's gifts to us.

TODAY'S VERSE

"As iron sharpens iron, so one man sharpens another" (Prov. 27:17).

EXAMINE

Soon after Bob professed faith in Christ, he attended a party-school kind of university. Because he was personable and outgoing, he made many friends. However, his new friends binged and engaged in lewd behavior. At first, Bob resisted the pressure to participate in their lifestyle, but he seemed to be a lone minnow in shark-infested water; so he succumbed to their influence, and wandered far from God.

> What a great favor God does to those he places in the company of good people.
>
> —Teresa of Avila

Todd, on the other hand, became a believer during his first year of college. A young Christian lady, whom he later married, led him to Christ. Immediately, Todd joined a Christian group on campus and a nearby Bible-believing church. His new friends helped him understand the Bible. They prayed with him, and supported him whenever his faith sagged. Today, Todd and his wife are missionaries in Europe.

It has been said that fellowship is fellows in the same ship. We should never underestimate the value of being onboard with the right friends.

EXPLORE

Evaluate your friendships. Are your closest friends Christians who help you to grow spiritually?

Are you helping them to grow spiritually?

If your circle of friends includes non-Christians, are you influencing them or vice versa?

EXERCISE

Get better acquainted with Christians in your social network. Invite them for coffee and a brief Bible study or prayer time.

> It is better to have one good friend than to have a good many bad friends.
>
> —author unknown

PRAY

Father, I ask you to enrich my life with good friends, and may I in turn enrich their lives.

Reinforcement

Accountable to God

ENGAGE

Each of us is directly accountable to God for how we live.

First Corinthians 4:1 states that Paul and his coworkers had been "entrusted with the secret things of God," and verse 2 teaches that all who have received a trust must demonstrate faithfulness. Paul honored the trust God had given him. Now it is our turn to be faithful, to realize that we are accountable to God.

TODAY'S VERSE

"So then, each of us will give an account of himself to God" (Rom. 14:12).

EXAMINE

Abraham had become wealthy, and his flocks and herds had multiplied greatly. So, he made his chief servant Eliezer the business manager of everything he possessed. This was an awesome responsibility, but he gave Eliezer an even bigger responsibility one memorable day. He made Eliezer vow that he would travel to Abraham's homeland and find a bride there for Abraham's son Isaac.

> The most important thought I ever had was that of my individual responsibility to God.
>
> —Daniel Webster

Finding a spouse for oneself is a huge task, but can you imagine how you would feel if your boss charged you with the job of finding a bride for his son? Eliezer performed his assignment admirably and brought back Rebekah, the perfect bride for Isaac.

Yes, he accomplished his mission because he felt accountable to Abraham, but it seems he felt even more accountable to God. Read the full story in Genesis 24, and note how he prayed for success, worshiped the Lord, praised him for his guidance, spoke of his kindness, and testified about his supervision of the mission.

If you perform your daily mission with a keen awareness of accountability to God, at the end of the day, you will be able to say, "Mission accomplished."

EXPLORE

No task is insignificant if it is what God wants you to do. If you perform it with a sense of accountability to him, he will reward you for work well done. How accountable to God do you see yourself in your daily tasks:

- Fully accountable?
- Somewhat accountable?
- Barely accountable?
- Not accountable?

> No task is insignificant if it is what God wants you to do and if you perform it with a sense of accountability to him.
>
> —author unknown

What difference will accountability to God make in the way you live today?

EXERCISE

Identify one responsibility you need to fulfill today. Fulfill it with a sense of full accountability to God. At the end of the day, indicate how faithfully you fulfilled the responsibility.

PRAY

Father, I cannot fulfill the responsibilities you have tailor-made for other believers, but with the help of the Holy Spirit I can fulfill the responsibilities you have given me. I am accountable to you, and I want to please you in all that I do today and every day.

Accountable to Others

ENGAGE

We are all accountable to somebody. At work, we are accountable to a supervisor or CEO or board of trustees. In our civil life, we are accountable to law enforcement and our authorities. In school, we are accountable to our teachers. In church, we are accountable to our elders. In sports, we are accountable to our coaches. Accountability is a way of life, and we would not fare very well without it; and having one or two good Christian friends who hold us accountable for our personal spiritual life is a priceless benefit.

Making ourselves accountable to others helps us be at our best for God.

TODAY'S VERSES

"Two are better than one, because they have a good return for their work: If one falls down, his friend can help him up. But pity the man who falls and has no one to help him up!" (Eccl. 4:9–10).

EXAMINE

Jim became a Christian when he was a teenager. His friend Ralph had recently become a Christian, and Ralph had profoundly influenced Jim's decision to believe in Christ as his Savior. Jim's family members did not attend church, but both friends knew they should attend. So they walked to church together, talked about what was going on in our lives, and prayed together. Although they didn't know what mutual accountability was, they practiced it.

> And let us consider how we may spur one another on toward love and good deeds.
>
> —Hebrews 10:24

Ralph would always greet Jim with the question, "How are things between your soul and the Creator?" From that point, they would share their victories and talk about their setbacks. If Jim needed correction or a gentle nudge to realign his steps with God's will, Ralph would supply it. Nothing was off limits for their frequent heart-to-heart discussions, and the mutual accountability spurred their growth. Jim was careful to maintain a steady fellowship with the Lord because he knew the next time he and Ralph met, Ralph would ask, "How are things between your soul and the Creator?"

EXPLORE

If you currently have one or two Christian friends who you hold accountable, how is that relationship helping you? What might strengthen the bonds of accountability?

EXERCISE

If you do not have one or two Christian friends to hold you accountable, contact one or more prospective accountability partners this week and establish an accountability relationship. If you have such a relationship, list a few concerns you should share.

PRAY

Father, I need reliable Christian friends who can hold me accountable for my spiritual development. Help me choose them wisely.

Day 3

Wanted:
Accountability Partner

We should look for a qualified accountability partner.

ENGAGE

Practice 6 in *ReThink Your Life* describes the qualities of a suitable accountability partner, whether in a one-on-one relationship or in a small group. A small group that exists in your church may serve you well if you have strong connections with the group's members and each person can freely open his or her life to the others. However, if such a group isn't available, you need to look for a qualified accountability partner.

TODAY'S VERSE

"Instead, speaking the truth in love, we will in all things grow up into him who is the Head, that is, Christ" (Eph. 4:15).

EXAMINE

Liz had not been a Christian long when she met Betty. Although Betty was about ninety, her mind was sharp and her love for God and his Word were apparent. Forty years younger than Betty, Liz wanted to grow spiritually and knew she needed an accountability partner. She was sure Betty was the right person for the job. Betty had a reputation for coming alongside women regardless of their ages and for treating them as equals in the quest for truth and spiritual maturity. She also was known for her honesty and willingness to listen without imposing strange beliefs on others. Furthermore, she was considered nonjudgmental. She could keep confidences, and she was loving, considerate, and always available to listen to others' concerns and ideas. And she prayed faithfully for her friends. So Liz asked Betty to be her accountability partner.

In addition to having someone cheer you on in your efforts, an accountability partner can also help trace your progress, making sure you stay on track.

Together, Liz and Betty shared their shortcomings, rejoiced in their victories, and prayed for increased spiritual wisdom and opportunities to share the good news of Christ. The partnership continued until Betty entered heaven, but she left Liz on earth better able to lead a strong Christian life.

EXPLORE

What do you want most from an accountability partnership?

What might you bring to that partnership?

How would you encourage a shy person to establish an accountability partnership?

EXERCISE

Write an imaginary ad to go in your church's newsletter, in which you advertise for a qualified accountability partner. Complete the wording that follows:

"Seeking accountability partner . . ."

PRAY

Father, help me establish a mutually beneficial accountability partnership. I want to grow stronger in my knowledge of your Word, to resist temptation, and to project a sincere and vibrant Christian testimony.

Accountability partners can share their shortcomings, rejoice in their victories, and pray for increased spiritual wisdom and opportunities to share the good news of Christ.

—author unknown

Day 4

Teach Us to Pray

Prayer is as essential
to the spirit as breathing
is to the body.

ENGAGE

Jesus' disciples asked of him many things but none more important than, "Lord, teach us to pray" (Luke 11:1). Learning to pray is basic to rethinking your life.

TODAY'S VERSE

"Do not be anxious about anything, but in everything, by prayer and petition, with thanksgiving, present your requests to God" (Phil. 4:6).

EXAMINE

George Mueller of England (1805–1898) relied on the power of prayer to keep his orphanages operating. One morning, the headmaster of one of the orphanages informed Mueller that the food supply had run out. Mueller urged the staff to pray. Within minutes, a milkman knocked at the door and reported that an axle on his wagon had broken, and he feared his milk, cheese, and eggs would spoil before the axle could be repaired. He asked whether the orphanage could use the food. Then a baker arrived and asked whether the orphanage could use his overload of bread and rolls.

Another time, when bills were due, the orphanage was two pennies short. George believed God wanted them to pay their bills in full, so he and the workers prayed. After a time of urgent prayer, they went to the donation box. Inside the box, two pennies were waiting for the prayerful workers.

George Mueller's life overflowed with stories of answered prayer.

> Pray as if everything depended upon your prayer.
> —William Booth

EXPLORE

What do you think prompted Jesus' disciples to ask Jesus to teach them to pray?

Have you considered asking someone to help you learn to pray?

If so, who would you consider an excellent teacher of prayer?

EXERCISE

Spend at least ten minutes in prayer today for others, perhaps for missionaries, lost individuals, sick people, your pastor, and family members.

PRAY

Father, help me to learn how to pray. Help me be diligent in praying for the needs of others.

Selfish Prayer

ENGAGE

Perhaps, when you were young, you sat on Santa's knee and told him what you wanted for Christmas. But eventually, you learned Santa is a fictional character and, therefore, you stopped asking him for things. Unlike Santa, God is real, and he grants our prayer requests if they are unselfish. As we rethink our lives, it is wise to rethink the motives and content of our prayers.

> "Gimme" prayers perceive God as merely a celestial Santa Claus.

TODAY'S VERSE

"When you ask, you do not receive, because you ask with wrong motives, that you may spend what you get on your pleasures" (James 4:3).

EXAMINE

When he launched his construction business, Bill asked his pastor to pray with him. In his prayer, Bill asked God to bless his new business venture, and he promised he would give God 10 percent of the company's profits.

As the business became successful, Bill faithfully donated 10 percent of the profits to the Lord's work. But eventually the business reached such a high plateau of success that 10 percent looked like an enormous amount of money. Bill met with his pastor again and asked him to pray with him. He explained his dilemma, "When I launched my business, the profits were small and so was the 10 percent, but now my business is booming, and 10 percent is a big chunk of money. Will you pray with me and ask the Lord to release me from my pledge to tithe?"

"I can't do that," the pastor answered, "but I can ask the Lord to shrink your business to the size it was when you felt good about tithing."

Selfish praying displeases God.

EXPLORE

Explore the motives behind your prayers. If they are selfish, ask for forgiveness, and rethink the meaning of prayer.

EXERCISE

Offer a prayer today in which you pray only for others.

PRAY

Father, I want my prayers to honor you and benefit others. Reveal any selfishness in what I say, and help me pray more like Jesus.

The Lord doesn't want us to think He is just the big 911 in the sky.

—Mike MacIntosh

Day 6

Unselfish Prayer

We should not only pray for ourselves but for other people as well.

ENGAGE

John 17, one of the longest chapters in the gospel of John, is, with the exception of the first verse, a prayer. It is Jesus' prayer for his disciples and by extension for us. We cannot follow Jesus' example well unless we pray unselfishly for others.

TODAY'S VERSE

"I urge, then, first of all, that requests, prayers, intercession and thanksgiving be made for everyone" (1 Tim. 2:1).

EXAMINE

Vera was wheelchair bound. Arthritis clamped down on her muscles like a vise. Pain wracked her body. She could hardly lift a fork without experiencing pain. But she always smiled through her tears.

There is a world of over six billion people out there, and we all could use someone in our corner, praying for us.

Vera, her mentally challenged brother, and her elderly mother lived in a starkly simple rental home that lacked running water. Yet, when her young pastor came to visit, he never heard a complaint from them. Vera would point out the morning newspaper's stories of accident victims, grieving families, and distressed individuals. "I prayed for this person today," she would say, "and I prayed for that person too." And then she would assure him she prayed every day for him and for the members of his small congregation.

That was Vera. She prayed daily for others, although her own needs could have captured her full attention. Her prayers were unselfish.

When Vera died, hundreds of strangers as well as those who knew her had lost a true friend.

EXPLORE

Recalling your most recent prayer, how many requests for others' needs did it contain?

Who needs your prayer support today?

Lord, help me live from day to day in such a self-forgetful way, that even when I kneel to pray, my prayer shall be for others.

—author unknown

EXERCISE

Call a few friends today, ask what prayer requests they have, and then present those requests to the Lord in prayer.

PRAY

Father, thank you for the people in my life that have been faithful to pray for me. Help me to be faithful to pray for those who need my prayers.

Exercise Your Mind

ENGAGE

Reportedly, a boy who loved chocolate visited a chocolate factory, where he climbed a ladder to look into a chocolate vat. He leaned in too far, and tumbled into the chocolate. "Lord," he prayed, "make me equal to this opportunity."

> When a person becomes a Christian, he doesn't throw away his mind, but opens it to the vast vistas of truths that stretch before him.

Vast opportunities to exercise the mind surround us. Are we equal to the opportunity?

TODAY'S VERSE

"Be transformed by the renewing of your mind. Then you will be able to test and approve what God's will is—his good, pleasing and perfect will" (Rom. 12:2).

EXAMINE

Rodin's famous sculpture, *The Thinker*, didn't just spring spontaneously from Rodin's hammer and chisel. As a young man, he worked for Varrier-Belleudse, who had a keen appreciation for new technologies that broadened Rodin's artistic horizons.

The medium is the message.

—Marshall McLuhan

In 1875, Rodin visited Italy, where Michelangelo's sculptures captured Rodin's imagination. Later, he familiarized himself with the so-called pre-Raphaelite painters. Influenced by the poet and artist William Blake, these painters had begun to illustrate Dante's literary works. Rodin also studied Blake's illustrations of Dante.

Commissioned by the French Government to create a portal for the entrance to the Museum of Decorative Art, Rodin called his work "The Gates of Hell" and drew about two hundred pieces for it, including *The Thinker*. It was supposed to be Dante contemplating Rodin's "The Gates of Hell."

Much stretching of the mind preceded Rodin's significant work, *The Thinker*, and much stretching of the mind through reading and pondering go into making us significant thinkers.

EXPLORE

What kinds of books do you most enjoy reading?

List the books you have read in the past three months.

What books will you read in the next three months?

What recent decision did you make after gathering as much relevant information as possible?

How will you improve your decision-making?

EXERCISE

Read the editorial page of today's newspaper. Put a checkmark next to the editorials and letters to the editor that you disagree with. Explain in writing or in conversation why you disagree with them.

Hastiness and superficiality are the psychic diseases of the twentieth century, and more than anywhere else this disease is reflected in the press.

—Alexander Solzhenitsyn

PRAY

Father, many media stimuli bombard me daily. Help me decide which messages I should accept as beneficial to my mental, emotional, and spiritual development.

Phase 4

Perseverance

Keep Your Eyes on the Goal

ENGAGE

Anyone who joins a weight-loss program knows the importance of establishing a goal and keeping it firmly in mind. Just a casual glance at a tempting dessert can prove not only distracting but also disastrous. Similarly, to reach a healthy life, we must keep our eyes focused on the goal.

We must never allow ourselves to get sidetracked from the goal of establishing the quality of life God wants us to achieve.

TODAY'S VERSE

"I press on toward the goal to win the prize for which God has called me heavenward in Christ Jesus" (Phil. 3:14).

EXAMINE

Michelle Akers took up soccer when she was eight years old and living in Seattle. As she grew, her love of soccer grew, and so did her soccer skills. Her goal was to be a champion soccer player.

Obstacles are those things you see when you take your eyes off the goal.

—Hannah More

Along the way to her goal, she received a scholarship to the University of Central Florida, where she became a four-time All-American. In 1988, she was named College Player of the Year. In 1991 and 1999, she played on the U.S. teams that won first FIFA World Cup, and in 1996, her U.S. team won an Olympic gold medal. In 2002, she was named FIFA Woman Player of the Century.

But it was not easy for Michelle to achieve her goal. She was diagnosed with Chronic Fatigue Syndrome in 1993. During her last World Cup appearance, she had to receive intravenous fluids after each game. Because she was receiving an IV, she almost missed the gold medal presentation. But she didn't; she had her eyes on the goal, and nothing would keep her from it.

EXPLORE

In your efforts to rethink your life, what are your short-term goals?

What are your long-term goals?

How determined are you to reach those goals in reliance on the Holy Spirit?

EXERCISE

Set an attainable spiritual goal for today. Reach that goal, and then thank God for his help in the process.

PRAY

Father, you do not want me to be stagnate in my Christian life. You want me to mature and become holy in thought and deed. Help me keep my eyes on the goal.

Give me a stock clerk with a goal and I'll give you a man who will make history. Give me a man with no goals and I'll give you a stock clerk.

—J. C. Penney

Never Give Up

Rethinking our lives
demands perseverance.

ENGAGE

Anyone who has followed a diet will admit to being tempted to return to eating unhealthy food. Perseverance is necessary if a dieter hopes to shed excess pounds and gain a new lease on life. Perseverance is also necessary if we hope to enjoy a strong, vibrant spiritual life.

TODAY'S VERSE

"Let us not become weary in doing good, for at the proper time we will reap a harvest if we do not give up" (Gal. 6:9).

EXAMINE

Eight weeks before he died of cancer in 1993, North Carolina State University basketball coach Jim Valvano (Jimmy V) gave an inspiring ESPY Awards speech. He announced the creation of the V Foundation for Cancer Research. He said the foundation's motto would be, "Don't give up. Don't ever give up."

Coach knew what perseverance was. In 1983, he inspired his North Carolina State Wolfpack team to battle against a more highly-ranked team and win the NCAA Championship. After the game, he ran up and down the court searching for someone to hug.

When a teleprompter at the ESPY Awards told him he had only thirty seconds to complete his speech, Coach Valvano observed: "That screen is flashing up there thirty seconds like I care about that screen right now, huh? I got tumors all over my body. I'm worried about some guy in the back going thirty seconds?" He closed the speech by saying, "Cancer can take away all my physical abilities. It cannot touch my mind, it cannot touch my heart, and it cannot touch my soul. And those three things are going to carry on forever. I thank you and God bless you all."*

EXPLORE

What challenges will you overcome today as you persevere in rethinking your life?

What advice would you give someone who seems to be giving up in his or her walk with the Lord?

EXERCISE

Tackle a spiritual discipline that seems difficult, perhaps prayer or Bible reading or resisting temptation, and persevere in that discipline today. At the end of the day, describe your victory in this journal.

PRAY

Father, strengthen my determination to never give up in the task of rethinking my life.

Don't give up.
Don't ever give up.

—Jim Valvano

NOTE

*The V Foundation for Cancer Research, "ESPY Awards Acceptance Speech," http://www.jimmyv.org/remembering-jim/espy-awards-speech.html (accessed May 27, 2010).

Day 3

Keep Learning

Like a garden, to be productive, the mind must be cultivated.

ENGAGE

Weeds grow without care, but we must expend energy and occasionally backbreaking effort to grow fruits, vegetables, and flowers. Nevertheless, the bounty and beauty of a well-tended garden make the effort worthwhile. It also requires effort to restrict weeds from our thought life and to increase the bounty and beauty of a productive mind.

TODAY'S VERSE

"When you come, bring the cloak that I left with Carpus at Troas, and my scrolls, especially the parchments" (2 Tim. 4:13).

EXAMINE

Nola Ochs graduated from Fort Hays State University in Hays, Kansas in 2007. But here's what made her graduation special: She was ninety-five years old at the time.

Nola doesn't believe in letting grass grow under her feet or moss cover her brain. Upon graduating, she said she wanted to be a storyteller on a cruise line and also continue her education. Shortly afterwards, Princess Cruises hired her as a guest lecturer. She accepted the offer and set sail on a nine-day Caribbean cruise.

Don't think Nola majored in basket weaving! She didn't. She was a history major, studied algebra, and maintained a 3.7 grade point average.

No doubt, Nola would agree that the mind is a terrible thing to waste.

The apostle Paul certainly didn't waste his mind. Although he was brilliant, he wanted to keep reading and learning, so he asked Timothy to bring "books" and Scriptures to him. He was in prison at the time and likely had plenty of time to read. He didn't want to squander the opportunity.

> You can be a lifetime learner right in the comfort of your very own home.

EXPLORE

Picture your mind as a garden. What is the greatest source of weeds you must guard against?

How well is the garden growing?

What can you do to speed the growth of your garden's beauty and quality?

EXERCISE

The mind is constituted of what it feeds on.

—author unknown

Refuse to watch TV this evening. Instead, read a section of the Bible, a literary classic, or a Christian book.

PRAY

Father, you have given me a sound mind. I dedicate it to you and ask you to help me develop my mind like a beautiful, bountiful garden.

Day 4

Don't Hesitate to Meditate

ENGAGE

Have you ever watched a cow chew grass? She doesn't simply bite a clump of grass and gulp it down in one quick motion. Not at all! She chews the grass, and chews it, and chews it some more. The motion is called rumination. When we chew slowly on God's Word, it's called meditation—and it's a good thing.

> Taking time to meditate in today's busy world provides relief from stress while reinforcing beneficial thoughts.

TODAY'S VERSE

"Oh, how I love your law! I meditate on it all day long" (Ps. 119:97).

EXAMINE

An interesting advertisement in the local newspaper caught my attention. It promised peace of mind and a sack lunch for just thirty-five dollars. I had to learn more, so I read the entire thing.

> People can't see your root system, but God can. Praying and meditating on the Word of God will cause your roots to go down deep into His love.
>
> —John Wesley

A back-to-nature group had placed the ad. The deal was this: Show up at a specific location outside a mountain town, and hand thirty-five dollars to the group's leader. In turn, she would hand you a sack lunch. Participants would hike barefoot along a mountain stream for an hour and then break for lunch. Hiking barefoot was supposed to put everyone in touch with nature. After lunch, everyone would pick up a stick from the ground, hike a short distance, and then sit on the ground and meditate, emptying the mind of all negative thoughts. Next, each person would mentally transfer his troubles to the stick he carried, toss his stick into the stream, and watch it carry away all his troubles.

Biblical meditation works differently. It has an object, God's Word; and it doesn't empty the mind, it fills it with God's thoughts.

We shouldn't hesitate to meditate, but we should meditate the right way.

EXPLORE

Read Psalm 119:165.

How can meditating on God's Word bring good balance to your life?

Does your Bible reading more closely resemble a cow ruminating or a pelican gulping?

EXERCISE

Meditate today on Philippians 4:1–8.

What truths come to mind from this passage that relate directly to your life?

PRAY

Father, your word nourishes my soul and guides my life. I will meditate upon it and relish the taste of it.

The Value of a
Discussion Group

A discussion can
provide social support,
stimulate learning, and
increase accountability.

ENGAGE

Psychiatrists, educators, and sociologists tout the benefits of small groups. Church leaders do too. No Christian needs to live as an island.

TODAY'S VERSE

"For waging war you need guidance, and for victory many advisers" (Prov. 24:6).

EXAMINE

Practice 9 in *ReThink Your Life* says: "The great value of a discussion group is that you can benefit from the thoughts, perspectives, and opinions of a group of people instead of just relying on your own insight" (p. 203).

Ron would agree wholeheartedly with that observation. Three years ago, he was a new believer struggling to understand the Bible and its relevance for everyday life. He became connected to a large church and appreciated the Sunday sermons, but he couldn't speak out in a worship service, state an opinion, or ask a question. So he kept his opinions and questions to himself.

> One of the most helpful ways to process the information in a book is to discuss it in a group.

One day, Ron decided to organize a discussion group. Others liked the idea, and soon about six to eight couples were meeting Sunday evenings for discussion. A few ground rules were put into place: no arguing, no such thing as a stupid question, everyone's comments would be respected, transparency and honesty would be valued, and confidences would be honored.

Now, three years later, Ron holds a leadership position in his church. He is a knowledgeable, exemplary believer, and a strong proponent of discussion groups.

EXPLORE

If you belong to a discussion group, how is the experience enriching your life?

If you do not belong to a discussion group, how might you start one?

If somebody comes to a neighborhood coffee hour, or goes to a discussion group, and they have a discussion, I do think that people really walk away with a real understanding of the issues.

—Mike Lowry

EXERCISE

What topic do you think would benefit members of a discussion group? Suggest that topic to your group leader. If you do not belong to a discussion group, contact several people about starting one.

PRAY

Father, help me listen well and speak wisely when I have an opportunity to participate in a discussion group.

Day 6

Embrace Technology

ENGAGE

Technology has taken giant strides in the past one hundred years. Homes used to share telephone party lines. Now nearly everyone carries a cell phone. The typewriter became a "dinosaur" and was replaced by the computer. Radios still exist, but TVs in high definition and hand-held wireless devices occupy our attention. Of course, some people fear change, but wouldn't they be happier and more productive if they joined the technology revolution?

Technology is neither moral nor immoral. We can use it for either good or evil, but we should not ignore it.

TODAY'S VERSE

"For God did not give us a spirit of timidity, but a spirit of power, of love and of self-discipline" (2 Tim. 1:7).

EXAMINE

Gloria, age seventy-four, used to question the purpose and need of a computer. "I have lived this long without one," she would say. "Why should I get a computer now?"

But she finally took a leap of faith and purchased a computer. Now she knows what she was a missing and wonders why she waited so long to tap into modern technology. She has met "old" friends on line, whom she e-mails daily. She posts photos and messages on Facebook, plays word games online, Tweets, and accesses Web sites that contain sermons and quotes of Bible teachers past and present. She shares what she considers the best sermons and quotes with her Facebook friends.

Using her cell phone, she also sends text messages to her children and grandchildren. Her digital camera allows her to take beautiful photos and transfer them to her computer.

Gloria is expanding the mind God gave her. She has become a virtual, female Buck Rogers—and she tries to persuade other senior citizens to stop feeling intimidated. "You would love using a computer," she tells them.

EXPLORE

What changes have you witnessed in your lifetime?

List the high-tech devices you use.

How have those devices enriched your life?

> Well informed people know it
> is impossible to transmit the
> voice over wires and that were
> it possible to do so, the thing
> would be of no practical value.
>
> —*The Boston Post*, 1865

EXERCISE

Visit a computer store or wireless phone store to discover what new devices are available to the communicating public. Stay alert to advances in technology.

PRAY

Father, enable me to make wise choices about technology. May I use technology to keep my mind active and serve you in new ways. May I be a constant learner, never paralyzed by fear.

Day 7

Stay Alive Until You Die

ENGAGE

As we rethink our lives, it is important not to dwell in the past but to anticipate the future and stay active in the present. We have all known retired persons whose health deteriorated because they chose to do little or nothing in the post-employment stage of life. Also, persons who are still employed can become bored if they come home from work, eat comfort food, and flop down in front of the TV.

God didn't intend for us to lead a boring life, but some individuals seem content to vegetate instead of percolate.

Grow old along
with me! The best
is yet to be.
—Robert Browning

TODAY'S VERSE

"The sluggard buries his hand in the dish; he will not even bring it back to his mouth!" (Prov. 19:24).

EXAMINE

If you visited Bailey and Alice more than a couple of times, you might be bored. That's because Bailey and Alice seem bored. Other than attending church on Sunday, they do nothing except watch TV until they fall asleep—she on the sofa, he in a recliner. They seldom talk to each other. When company arrives, they rehearse past events from their fifty-eight years of marriage—where they lived, what they did during World War II, their surgeries, and ubsequent aches and pains. They follow the same script every time they have visitors. Apparently, nothing interesting is happening in the present or is about to happen in the future.

Steve and Betty have been married sixty-four years. They captivate visitors with their lively conversations. They laugh often, discuss current news events, kid each other about their bowling scores, and never complain.

Bailey and Alice vegetate; Steve and Betty percolate. And life pays back what each couple puts into it.

EXPLORE

Review your past week. Did you rejoice more than complain?

Does it seem that people genuinely like to spend time with you?

What new hobbies and interests have you pursued this year?

EXERCISE

Adopt one new hobby or interest and pursue it with a positive attitude.

Old age is a part of life, and it can be the best part.

—author unknown

PRAY

Father, I want to explore new opportunities to stretch my mind and enrich my life. Lead me in exciting paths.

Research

ENGAGE

When a hurricane develops over the Atlantic, meteorologists turn to their favorite hurricane expert for his opinion about its force, path, and projected landfall. The expert didn't gain his knowledge overnight; he zeroed in on his topic and studied it in depth for years.

Many people seem to know a little about everything, whereas some people seem to know everything about something.

TODAY'S VERSE

"Therefore, since I myself have carefully investigated everything from the beginning, it seemed good also to me to write an orderly account for you, most excellent Theophilus" (Luke 1:3).

EXAMINE

Brian knows more about frogs than you can probably imagine. His interest in these slimy amphibians began when he was nine. His family took a trip to Oregon, where Brian caught some tadpoles. He insisted on putting them in a bucket of water and transporting them back home.

Brian bought books about frogs and pored over them intensely. Before long, he could identify each type of frog and its habitat. His frog research took him to pet stores, where he purchased a few frogs. But not all pet stores sold exotic frogs, so Brian researched the Internet for dealers of exotic frogs. Some dealers exhibited at reptile shows; others at exotic pet stores. Eventually Brian was the proud owner of 102 frogs. Most of them ate crickets and mealworms, but at least one dined on mice.

EXPLORE

What hobbies or areas of interest do you specialize in?

How would you describe your study habits?

Respond to the following statement: "I studied enough in school. Now that I am an adult, I don't have to study."

What really gets your blood pumping? What can you see yourself getting out of bed early on Saturday morning for?

EXERCISE

Choose a topic you would like to explore in depth. Begin to research it on the Internet and at the library.

PRAY

Father, I don't want my mind to stagnate. The world you created has so many interesting features. Help me explore one new feature in depth.

Tone Those Muscles

ENGAGE

At daybreak, before they begin their workday, exercise enthusiasts work out. They may visit a gym and lift weights or use a treadmill, or they may prefer to walk or jog outdoors. They know a fit body contributes to good health and improved quality of life.

> The body is the temple of the Holy Spirit. Shouldn't we take good care of it?

TODAY'S VERSE

"Do you not know that your body is a temple of the Holy Spirit, who is in you, whom you have received from God?" (1 Cor. 6:19).

Good health always seems more valuable after we lose it.

—author unknown

EXAMINE

Terry hadn't bothered to take care of himself. He ate wrong and seldom exercised. As he approached retirement, his weight escalated and his blood pressure elevated. Then, one day, as he was talking to a coworker, his vision blurred, he grew dizzy, and a numbness overtook the left side of his body. He had suffered a stroke, what the neurologist would call a lacunar infarction.

Terry was put on blood thinners and advised to lose weight and exercise. "Unless you get your blood pressure under control," the neurologist warned, "you are at risk for a big stroke."

As a Christian, Terry had always believed his body was a temple of the Holy Spirit, but that belief had never taken hold as it did after he suffered a stroke. As soon as he was strong enough, he walked around his neighborhood block. And then, as he was able, he extended the distance. Now, he walks two miles daily, and he has joined a YMCA. He has lost weight, eats right, and his blood pressure is normal.

Terry is keeping the temple of the Holy Spirit in good condition.

EXPLORE

Why is it important to keep your body in good condition?

Why do you agree or disagree that Christians should eat right and exercise?

Do you have an annual physical examination? Why or why not?

> A man's health can be judged by which he takes two at a time—pills or stairs.
>
> —Joan Welsh

EXERCISE

Pay attention to food labels. If you have been careless about what you eat, change your eating habits starting today. Begin an exercise program today, or extend your current program.

PRAY

Father, I dedicate my body to you. I will take care of it and use it to serve you.

Those Crazy Thoughts

We need to bid farewell to unfounded thoughts before they defeat us.

ENGAGE

Thoughts are powerful. As we rethink our lives, we need to examine thoughts we entertain that have no basis in fact. For example, if we think we are worthless, we may find it difficult to do the worthwhile things God wants us to accomplish.

TODAY'S VERSE

"We take captive every thought to make it obedient to Christ" (2 Cor. 10:5).

EXAMINE

It's possible to hold thoughts that have no basis in reality. They cause us to fear, and they may even keep us from doing what we need to do. We need to identify those thoughts and take them captive for Christ.

The preacher's voice had become faint. And then, during a Sunday morning sermon, it quit altogether. Various therapies and medications failed to restore the preacher's voice, but finally a doctor discovered the source of the malady — an allergy. It seems the preacher slept with his bedroom window open, and a bed of mums lay just outside the window. At the doctor's suggestion, the preacher removed the mums, and *presto* his voice returned.

> To the timid and hesitating everything is impossible, because it seems so.
>
> —Sir Walter Scott

All went well until the preacher was the guest speaker for a distant church. His voice faded to nothing. Looking down at a table of mums in front of the pulpit, he motioned to ushers to carry the flowers away. As soon as the flowers had been removed, his voice returned.

After the service, an usher explained, "Preacher, those were artificial flowers on the table."

EXPLORE

What thought or thoughts have kept you from accomplishing a task you wanted to begin? How worried are you about something that may never happen?

If anything can bring your fears to pass, it will be your worries.

—author unknown

EXERCISE

Write down one or two thoughts that you will take captive for Christ right now.

PRAY

Father, help me focus my mind on what is true and constructive and expunge harmful thoughts from my mind.

What Disability?

ENGAGE

A false self-image may keep us from accomplishing God's will. If we think we are not good enough, smart enough, or talented enough, we will never lead the life he wants us to enjoy.

Nothing is too hard for God.

TODAY'S VERSE

"For you created my inmost being; you knit me together in my mother's womb. I praise you because I am fearfully and wonderfully made; your works are wonderful, I know that full well" (Ps. 139:13–14).

EXAMINE

Being paralyzed below the neck didn't stop Dave from taking on big projects.

He accepted a Sunday school teaching assignment and performed so well that his young adult class became extremely popular. He studied an advanced Bible correspondence course. He attended university, where he earned a Bachelor of Arts and a Master of Arts in Business. He launched a successful insurance business, and he even ran for the office of state representative.

Doctors had predicted Dave would not live beyond the teenage years, but he lived past sixty. His mind was sharp. His relationship with the Lord was exemplary. And his approach to life was positive. Those who were close to Dave said he never complained—not even once.

EXPLORE

What have you accomplished recently with the Lord's help?

Why should a believer refuse to complain when life seems hard?

EXERCISE

Get out if your comfort zone! Do something new and challenging.

PRAY

Father, help me turn my inability or disability over to you. May your ability be my strength.

God is faithful and will always be there when you need him.

Day 12

Of Marigolds and Ragweed

Can you distinguish marigolds from ragweed or truth from error?

ENGAGE

Just because an attractive, smooth-talking, acclaimed TV anchor reports a story, it doesn't mean the story is true. It may be partly true or completely false. We need to think critically about what so-called authorities say.

TODAY'S VERSE

"Dear friends, do not believe every spirit, but test the spirits to see whether they are from God, because many false prophets have gone out into the world" (1 John 4:1).

EXAMINE

Practice 8 in *ReThink Your Life* encourages us to improve our higher thinking skills by thinking critically (p. 184). Thinking critically compels us to separate reality from fiction, fact from rumor, and truth from error.

A man had planted marigold seeds in a window box. He watered the seeds faithfully, and enjoyed watching the seeds become tiny shoots and eventually blooming marigolds. But several shoots bore no flowers. He wondered why until someone asked, "Why are you growing ragweed in your window box?"

> Once we discard the illusion that the mass media offer us an objective, transparent view of reality, we can begin to have confidence in our own perceptions and judgments.
>
> —James McDowell

The problem is that ragweed and marigolds look alike in the early stages of their growth. Without this knowledge, he was devoting time and energy to a very nasty form of plant life.

Do we recognize the difference between truth and error? If we do not, we may ignorantly contribute to error's growth.

EXPLORE

Briefly list teachings about God, the Bible, Jesus, and the Holy Spirit that you know are true.

How would you respond if someone knocked on your door and said Jesus was merely an angel who became a man?

EXERCISE

Next time you read a newspaper, employ critical thinking. Mark a T for true or an F for false beside each editorial and letter to the editor.

PRAY

Father, teach me your truth. Help me improve my critical thinking so I can avoid error.

Down with Anger

ENGAGE

Righteous indignation is a good thing, but anger that flies off the handle or takes matters into one's own hands is unrighteous. Anger management classes may be the answer for some, but rethinking our life as a believer is helpful more as a lasting solution.

When a man loses his temper, it reveals the worst part of him.

TODAY'S VERSE

"'In your anger do not sin': Do not let the sun go down while you are still angry" (Eph. 4:26).

EXAMINE

Two pastors saw red whenever they met. The heated words they exchanged in public embarrassed everyone within earshot. Nobody knew why each man was angry with the other. Even the two pastors had long since forgotten the reason, but their anger remained as hot as soup boiling on a stove.

One night, after a pastors' conference, each of the two went to a private residence to which he had been assigned. Each man was escorted separately to a guest room. Soon, the two were together in the same room and staring down at a double bed that sagged in the middle. The anger gave way to laughter. "Brother," one said to the other, "if we hope to get any sleep, we had better reconcile and ask the Lord to forgive us."

As the two knelt for prayer, anger left the room.

EXPLORE

What seems to make you angry?

How do you usually handle anger?

What difference do you see between righteous indignation and sinful anger?

EXERCISE

Contact someone with whom you have been angry. Ask for his or her forgiveness.

PRAY

Father, I recall that Jesus responded to angry men by praying for their forgiveness. Help me not to repay anger with anger but to extend forgiveness.

Anger makes you smaller, while forgiveness forces you to grow beyond what you were.

—Cherie Carter-Scott

Day 14

Transfer the Title Deed

Life takes significance and beauty when we transfer the title deed to the Lord.

ENGAGE

If someone handed you the title deed to a house, you would become the owner. You could paint the house whatever color you wished, and you could even remodel the whole house to your liking. When we give the Lord the title deed to our bodies, we acknowledge we are his to use as he desires.

TODAY'S VERSE

"Therefore, I urge you, brothers, in view of God's mercy, to offer your bodies as living sacrifices, holy and pleasing to God—this is your spiritual act of worship" (Rom. 12:1).

EXAMINE

In his book, *My Heart, Christ's Home*, author Robert Boyd Munger pictures a visit from Jesus to his home. He escorts Jesus to the various rooms: the study, the living room, the dining room, etc., but it became apparent that Jesus was not pleased with everything. The hall closet, for example, needed a thorough cleaning. Convinced that Jesus could transform the whole house, the narrator hurries to transfer the title deed to Jesus.

Is Jesus waiting for you and me to transfer the title deed to him?

> We owe God nothing less than our all.
>
> —author unknown

EXPLORE

Take an inventory of your life. What parts of your life do you need to offer Jesus:

- Your social life?

- Your recreational life?

- Your study life?

EXERCISE

Draft a simple title deed in which you transfer all your body and life to Jesus. Sign and date it.

He is no fool
who gives up
what he cannot
keep to gain what
he cannot lose.

—Jim Elliot

PRAY

Father, please take possession of all I am and have. Remodel my entire life so the beauty of Jesus will be seen in me.

Self-Denial

ENGAGE

Jesus instructed us to "enter through the narrow gate" (Matt. 7:13). He said the wide gate opens into a broad road that leads to destruction. However, the narrow gate opens to a narrow road that leads to life. Many make the mistake of choosing to pass through the wide gate.

God gives his best to those who deny self and walk the straight and narrow road.

TODAY'S VERSE

"But small is the gate and narrow the road that leads to life, and only a few find it" (Matt. 7:14).

EXAMINE

Practice 9 of *ReThink Your Life* tells us: "Our culture is continually telling us to travel the broad road, to walk through the wide gate, to make the easiest choice and put ourselves first. But that path only leads to destruction" (p. 211).

The narrow road is always a choice you can make.

If you visit the Rocky Mountains, you can choose to follow roads most tourists take. The popular interstates and state highways don't require much maneuvering. Nor do they jostle drivers and passengers. But if you really want to capture the thrill of viewing panoramic vistas, wildlife, deep gorges, and plunging streams, rent a jeep, and follow narrow trails, some of which used to be stagecoach trails.

To view life at its best—abundant, spectacular life—get out of the world's parade, and follow Jesus along the narrow road.

EXPLORE

Describe a time when you followed a narrow road, literally or philosophically, and it led to a wonderful experience.

Why is the wide road so attractive to so many people?

EXERCISE

Invite a non-Christian friend for coffee, and describe for him or her a few benefits of following the narrow road.

The Savior's hand is better than a map, for it upholds while it guides.

—author unknown

PRAY

Father, help me show someone the narrow gate today.

Day 16

God Created the One and Only You

Even identical twins are not identical, because each one is God's distinct creation.

ENGAGE

The evolutionist sees you and himself as a product of chance and a testament to the survival of the fittest. However, the Bible teaches that you are God's distinctly designed creation.

TODAY'S VERSE

"Then God said, 'Let us make man in our image, in our likeness'" (Gen. 1:26).

EXAMINE

When a penny is minted, Abraham Lincoln's image is stamped on it. The image bears witness to the fact that the penny is an American penny. When God created Adam and Eve, the first human beings, he stamped his image in them. They reflected the nature of the creator. Although God created everything else, he did not create anything except human beings in his image. So you are distinct, one of a kind.

Your DNA is distinct. Your finger-prints are distinct. Your eye scan is distinct. Your self-concept is distinct. The plan God has for your life is distinct! And your spirit sets you apart from all animal life.

> Just because you made a mistake doesn't mean you are a mistake.
>
> —Georgette Mosbacher

So next time you look at a penny, remind yourself that God has stamped his image in you.

EXPLORE

List some way you are different from your closest relative. What value do you hold in God's sight?

EXERCISE

Complete the following statement: Because I bear the image of God, today I will . . .

You . . . crowned
him with glory
and honor.

—Psalm 8:5

PRAY

Father, you created me for your glory. Help me fulfill that purpose today.

Day 17

In Good Hands

ENGAGE

The God who loves us keeps us safe.

The world can be a very unsafe place. Criminals and terrorists may strike anywhere and anytime. However, the believer can take refuge "in the shelter of God's tabernacle" (Ps. 27:5).

TODAY'S VERSE

"He will hide me in the shelter of his tabernacle and set me high upon a rock" (Ps. 27:5).

EXAMINE

A golf course is an enjoyable place on a sunny, cloudless day, but it can be a hazardous place when the sky darkens and lightning rips across the sky. Metal golf clubs attract lightning as surely as a picnic attracts ants. Lightning can kill unwary golfers.

The United States Air Force Academy's two golf courses are located in the foothills near Pikes Peak. Late day summer thunderstorms often roll off the Rockies and onto the golf courses suddenly and ferociously, but the Academy's warning system alerts golfers of approaching lightning in time for them to take shelter and wait out the storm.

Anyone who has played at the Academy when the warning sounds can appreciate the availability of the courses' shelters. But we can be even more thankful for the fact that God is the ultimate shelter in life's storms.

EXPLORE

How has the Lord shown you that he is a safe shelter?

What "storms" are threatening your life today?

How does it help to know the Lord has sheltered you in the past?

EXERCISE

Identify a threatening situation and commit
yourself to the Lord for safekeeping.

PRAY

Father, you are my shelter. As I rethink
my life, may I possess comforting thoughts about your protection.

Even though I walk
through the valley of
the shadow of death,
I will fear no evil, for
you are with me.

—Psalm 23:4

Day 18

Better than GPS

God guides his
children all the
days of their lives.

ENGAGE

If we want to know how to get from Point A to Point B, we can consult the Internet and receive clear directions and even a map. Finding our way through life demands guidance from God, who is an even more reliable source than a GPS.

TODAY'S VERSE

"For this God is our God for ever and ever; he will be our guide even to the end" (Ps. 48:14).

EXAMINE

Have you ever found yourself lost in the middle of an unfamiliar city, with no landmarks or knowledge to guide your way? Maybe you forgot to take a map or decided not to look up directions because the person you were with supposedly knew where he or she was going.

> It is difficult to steer a parked car, so get it moving.
> —Henrietta Mears

Today, many people are able to quickly extract themselves from such sticky situations using a portable GPS (Global Positioning System). You probably know that these devices use the latest technology to locate your whereabouts as well as your desired destination. This device will then construct the best pathway for you to get from one location to another. Some of the devices even have the option to distinguish if you want a male or female voice that calmly and authoritatively tells you what your next turn or step should be.

A GPS is valuable, but God's guidance system is even better. He guides us perfectly through trials and decision-making times. All we have to do is give him control of our lives.

EXPLORE

What situations are you facing that call for decisions?

How has God's guidance in the past prepared you for future decisions?

Men give advice;
God gives guidance.

—Leonard Ravenhill

EXERCISE

Pray for guidance as you make an important decision today. Make the decision when God's peace settles over your mind and heart.

PRAY

Father, guide me today, and give me the wisdom to see your hand in every decision.

Day 19

Be an Encourager

ENGAGE

As we rethink our lives, shouldn't we examine our relationships? Do we discourage others or encourage them? Do we block their path when they hope to achieve something great, or do we affirm them and assure them they will be successful?

A person may go far after receiving a pat on the back.

TODAY'S VERSE

"What, then, shall we say in response to this? If God is for us, who can be against us?" (Rom. 8:31).

EXAMINE

The book, *Three Thousand Illustrations for Christian Service*, includes an inspiring story about Sir Walter Scott. Apparently, as a schoolboy, he spent much of his time in the dunce's corner. However, his work ethic changed dramatically when he was a young teenager and met Robert Burns, Scotland's beloved poet.

Scott encountered Burns admiring a picture and an inscribed couplet. Scott drew alongside Burns, and whispered the name of the couplet's author, and then quoted the couplet. Impressed, Burns placed his hand on Scott's head and exclaimed, "Ah, bairnie, ye will be a great mon yet in Scotland some day!"

That word of encouragement started Walter Scott on the road to success.

EXPLORE

What encouragement have you received recently?

What encouragement have you given recently?

What thoughts about God's character encourage you?

EXERCISE

Send a note of encouragement to someone today. Perhaps a young child needs your encouragement.

When everything seems to be going against you, remember that the airplane takes off against the wind, not with it.

—Henry Ford

PRAY

Father, I want to encourage people. Help me to speak words that uplift instead of tear down.

Day 20

TV or Not TV?
That Is the Question

ENGAGE

If we fail to use TV properly, it may abuse us.

In its early days, TV offered limited viewing, and most of what it offered was family-oriented and wholesome. But today's TV may include hundreds of channels with programs, including G-rated ones and X-rated ones. As we rethink our lives, we must evaluate our TV viewing.

TODAY'S VERSE

"Finally, brothers, whatever is true, whatever is noble, whatever is right, whatever is pure, whatever is lovely, whatever is admirable— if anything is excellent or praiseworthy—think about such things" (Phil. 4:8).

EXAMINE

Don seemed unable to control his TV viewing, especially Saturdays, when so many movies flashed onto the screen. He would watch a matinee movie, then an early evening movie, then a prime-time movie, then a late-night movie, then a midnight movie, and then fall asleep in his recliner.

He hadn't revealed his TV addiction to his Christian friends because he was a Sunday school teacher. However, one Sunday, as he began his class, his secret surfaced. He asked his students to open their Bibles to John, channel 4.

Don's problem was not that he owned a TV but that the TV owned him. We don't have to set the TV on the curb for the trash men to haul away, but we do need to monitor our viewing. We can choose to watch what is uplifting, family-oriented, and educational. If Don follows a regimen of watching carefully selected TV programs, he will be a better-rested and better-informed teacher.

> All television is educational. The question is: What is it teaching?
>
> —Nicholas Johnson

EXPLORE

On average, how much time each day do you spend watching TV?

What have you seen recently that truly engaged your mind and informed you?

What have you seen recently that embarrassed you?

I have never seen a bad television program, because I refuse to. God gave me a mind, and a wrist that turns things off.

—Jack Paar

EXERCISE

Make a copy of the Media Inventory Worksheet found on page 236 of *ReThink Your Life*. Use it as instructed on page 235. For an even broader application of today's meditation, use the Media Meal Plan Worksheet given on page 238.

PRAY

Father, may my ears and eyes be closed to media messages that hinder my relationship with you. Help me focus on what is beneficial.

The Indispensable Holy Spirit

ENGAGE

Jesus promised his followers that the Comforter would come to them and guide them into all truth. The Counselor (Paraclete) is the Holy Spirit who has been called alongside us to encourage and promote holiness in us. We must not rethink our lives without relying on the Spirit's wisdom and strength.

The Holy Spirit plays an indispensable role in the rethinking of our lives.

TODAY'S VERSE

"But the Counselor, the Holy Spirit, whom the Father will send in my name, will teach you all things and will remind you of everything I have said to you" (John 14:26).

EXAMINE

Evangelist Vance Havner (1901–1986) told the story of a group of boys that wanted to play baseball one afternoon. They designated two boys to take turns choosing team members. When the teams were in place, a boy called out, "Play ball!"

"Who brought a ball?" another asked.

There was total silence until several voices chorused, "We don't have a ball."

> The Spirit is closer than breathing, nearer than hands and feet.
>
> —author unknown

"Forget the ball," one boy shouted, "let's just get on with the game."

Of course, a ball is indispensable to a baseball game, and the Holy Spirit is indispensable to a productive and joyful Christian life. If we try to lead an abundant life without relying on the Holy Spirit, we will fail, but he is pleased to empower us as we rely on him.

EXPLORE

How heavily do you depend on the Holy Spirit for wisdom?

Have you experienced the sanctifying power of the Holy Spirit in your life?

If so, how did he manifest his power?

> Too common is the sin of forgetting the Holy Spirit, of grieving him by slights and neglect.
>
> —author unknown

EXERCISE

Read Galatians 5:22–23. Which quality mentioned in these verses seems most lacking in your life? Depend on the Holy Spirit to cultivate this quality in your life, and then perform at least one deed that evidences this quality.

PRAY

Father, thank you for sending the Holy Spirit to help me lead a life that pleases you and blesses others. I yield my heart and will to the Holy Spirit so that I may become more like Jesus.

Journal

Journal

Journal

Journal

Journal

Journal